THE
POWER

OF
PENTECOST

Discover and experience the truth
of what God intended for Pentecost!

BY MORRIS CERULLO

Morris Cerullo World Evangelism
P.O. Box 85277
San Diego, CA 92186

Morris Cerullo World Evangelism of Canada
P.O. Box 3600
Concord, Ontario L4K 1B6

Morris Cerullo World Evangelism of Great Britain
P.O. Box 277
Hemel Hempstead, Herts HP2 7DH

1st Printing 2014

Published by Morris Cerullo World Evangelism
Copyright © 2014
San Diego, California
Printed in the United States of America.

ISBN: 978-1-932579-38-3

TABLE OF
CONTENTS

You Kippur
Oct 3rd 2014

INTRODUCTION

Friend, do you want to experience a renewal of the power of Pentecost the same as when God literally breathed down spiritual fire in the Upper Room? Then get ready to go past the point of blessing to experience the fullness of God's power.

But ye shall receive power, after that the Holy Ghost is come upon you: ...

Acts 1:8

You, too, can experience the fire of the Holy Spirit burning within! One hundred and twenty of Jesus' closest disciples were praying fervently in the Upper Room when the Holy Spirit fell upon them in Acts, Chapter 2.

God wants to pour out His Spirit upon your life—perhaps like you have never experienced before. That's why I am so excited to share this revelation with you.

God commanded in His Word that we celebrate three feasts. He instructs us to celebrate all three of them. These appointed feasts are: the Feast of Passover, the Feast of Pentecost, and the Feast of Tabernacles.

God has promised that He would do something incredibly special when we are obedient to partake in these feasts the way He commanded us. This will be a blessing—a miracle outpouring—and a fulfillment so rich that you cannot even grasp its totality.

Pentecost is a special season, a time when God desires His people to experience a powerful release. Jesus told His disciples,

... tarry ye in the city of Jerusalem, until ye be endued with power from on high.

Luke 24:49

This powerful promise preceded the receiving of the Holy Spirit. Because of their obedience, the one hundred and twenty believers who tarried in the Upper Room were baptized in the Holy Spirit.

As you yield yourself and obey God's Word, He is going to baptize you as well! God uses the season and celebration of Pentecost to RELEASE!

As you read this book, embrace its powerful truths, and apply them to your life. I believe that as you do, every aspect of your life, your family, and your ministry will be turned right-side-up by an overwhelming overflow of Holy Ghost FIRE!

Beloved, we are entering into the fulfillment of the prophecy given by God through His prophet Joel, and quoted here by Peter on the day of Pentecost:

atonement

And it shall come to pass in the last days, saith God, I will pour out of my Spirit upon all flesh: and your sons and your daughters shall prophesy, and your young men shall see visions, and your old men shall dream dreams: And on my servants and on my handmaidens I will pour out in those days of my Spirit; and they shall prophesy:

Acts 2:17-18

Be obedient today. Position yourself to receive like never before!

God's servant,

Morris Cerullo

viii

CHAPTER ONE

BREAKTHROUGH FOR GOD'S PEOPLE!

Would you like to know one of the greatest spiritual secrets that has the potential to change the entire world? **The Church cannot change the world until we become a changed people.** We must seek after a unique characteristic—the special ingredient that gave birth to the Early Church.

All truth is parallel. You and I live in a natural world, but we also live in another world. Man has two sets of ears. Yes, he has these natural ears; but, he also has spiritual ears. He also has two sets of eyes; he has natural vision and spiritual eyesight.

In the past seventy-five years, we have made more breakthroughs in this natural world than in all of history put together. Daniel prophesied that this phenomenon would come to pass. He said that man's knowledge would increase. It cannot be denied that we are making major, critical breakthroughs in the natural world, but what is happening to us spiritually? Is the Church making the same breakthroughs spiritually that the world is making? The answer is clearly, "No!"

What has happened to the Church of the Living God? What has happened to the living, moving body of believers that was born in an explosion of spiritual power?

Didn't Jesus say that the gates of hell would not be able to prevail against His Church? What has happened to the spiritual kingdom that Jesus established, and Daniel prophesied would one day take dominion over the earth?

And in the days of these kings shall the God of heaven set up a kingdom, which shall never be destroyed: and the kingdom shall not be left to other people, but it shall break in pieces and consume all these kingdoms, and it shall stand for ever

Daniel 2:44

A huge part of this problem is the fact that the Church has de-emphasized the reality and actual demonstration of the Holy Spirit.

You may ask, *What are you saying, Brother Cerullo?*

I'm saying that people have gotten satisfied with just being 'blessed'. However, that is NOT all that God intended to do for us. He wants us to go PAST the point of blessing.

This is much more than you just going up to a prayer line and experiencing a good feeling. God wants to do a NEW WORK in your life! He wants you to experience a fresh, NEW ANOINTING! He wants to give you NEW MANNA! He wants to give you a NEW VISION ... NEW REVELATION ... and a NEW, SPIRITUAL UNDERSTANDING concerning His plan and purpose for your life in this end-time hour.

Perhaps you may feel like you are at a weak point in your Christian journey. You may be experiencing battle fatigue; Satan has tried to steal the peace and joy you once felt within. You are having a difficult time fighting Satan's attacks on your body, your finances, and your family. The spiritual battles have been hot and heavy.

Some of you have even experienced major setbacks in your finances ... large hospital and doctor bills. Some of you have suffered physically so long you have said to yourself, I just don't know how I can make it another day! Others of you have been praying and believing for many years for God to intervene in the circumstances of your loved ones.

I encourage you to hold on! The end is not yet! On the other side of your circumstances awaits a spiritual truth that has the powerful potential to totally transform the situations in your life that are bringing you down.

What are the battles that you are facing right now? Are there problems in your finances? Are there problems in your family or marriage? Are there areas in your life that you need to surrender to God? Are there stressful situations on your job? Are you wedged between personal struggles and spiritual battles?

God has not planned for you to be defeated in any of these circumstances. He has planned for you to have spiritual conquests and victories. But, you will never defeat these circumstances in your own strength and ability.

We cannot receive what God has for us until God gives us a breakthrough in our understanding of the Holy Spirit and God's intimate power.

A breakthrough is a sudden burst of advanced knowledge that takes us past a line of defense. If we do not experience another wave of Pentecost ... if we do not experience the genuine reality of the infilling of the Holy Ghost into the lives of God's army right now ... there will be no hope for this world!

The Holy Spirit has spoken: **There is coming an awesome, incredible, new wave of revival, of the biblical Pentecost that happened over 2,000 years ago, when the sound of a rushing, mighty wind came and filled the place, and cloven tongues of fire broke out!**

Once you engage in this same experience, the POWER OF GOD will then flow into your life as a result of this encounter with the person of the Holy Spirit. *I declare today, that you are going to receive POWER, because you are going to experience the baptism of the Holy Spirit.*

The PURPOSE of you experiencing this infilling of God's Spirit is not just to make you feel good. It's not sent primarily to bless you, alone. *Rather, God is going to baptize you in the Holy Spirit in order for you to work the works of God in your sphere of influence.* For example, if you are a nurse, God intends for you to share this revelation with the other medical staff in the hospital where you work. It's not to be kept to yourself. This is how the world will be changed!

A new revelation of your responsibility as a minister will completely flood your understanding. Without this revelation and breakthrough experience of POWER, you will not have the resources or ability to be the witness who God's Word has commissioned you to be!

Jesus said ... *greater works than these shall he do; because I go unto my Father* (John 14:12). God is calling you to experience a tremendous BREAKTHROUGH and the Holy Spirit is your key to that breakthrough. My prayer is that through this book, God—through His Spirit—will lead you into these greater works.

CHAPTER TWO

YE SHALL RECEIVE POWER!

For many years, the charismatic Church has emphasized the experience of tongues. I believe in speaking in other tongues. Even Paul said, *I thank my God, I speak with tongues more than ye all:* (I Corinthians 14:18).

The Bible says, *For he that speaketh in an unknown tongue speaketh not unto men but unto God ...* (I Corinthians 14:2). But watch people who are trying to receive the baptism of the Holy Spirit.

We've been taught that when we receive the experience of tongues that we receive the baptism of the Holy Ghost. We teach all of these people to seek the Lord until they speak in other tongues. When that experience comes, you have the baptism.

I used to teach that too! I taught that for years, until God gave me a breakthrough in power. Then, I was able to understand through revelation for the first time in my life what the Baptism of the Holy Spirit really is.

I can't relegate what we know as the force that gave the Church the divine ingredient that enabled it to reach the world. It wasn't tongues. It was POWER—a manifestation of Pentecostal power

Something happened to the disciples in the Early Church. On the day of Pentecost, when the Holy Spirit came to dwell within them, they were changed! (Read more about this Holy-Spirit-empowered Church from on high in the Pentecost Bible study on page 41). It was more than a celebration ... more than just speaking in unknown tongues ... more than an emotional experience. It was more than laughing in the Spirit, being slain in the Spirit, or any other outward manifestation.

To fully grasp this power, one must go beyond seeking an outward manifestation, BEYOND the point of blessing. They were baptized—completely submerged into one with God—where they totally possessed the Spirit without measure.

Peter wasn't the same man who had been running and hiding from the cross. Peter was not the same man who had denied Jesus. He was a new man ... a changed man walking in the unlimited power of God with incredible boldness that enabled him to reach down to the lame man and say, ... *Silver and gold have I none; but such as I have give I thee: In the name of Jesus Christ of Nazareth rise up and walk* (Acts 3:6).

The key to the release of the power of God in the lives of the disciples was that they waited before God in His presence with the expectation of the fulfillment of the promise. When they entered into the upper room, their hearts and minds were focused upon the promise Jesus had given them concerning the coming of the Holy Spirit. *But ye shall receive power, after that the Holy Ghost is come upon you:* (Acts 1:8).

They did not have any preconceived ideas concerning what would happen or how God would manifest His power in their lives. They did not place any limitations upon God. They were totally yielded and ready to receive the experience God had promised.

I am often asked, *Papa, what happened to the true manifestation of the power of Pentecost?* During the first few centuries, the Church experienced its greatest growth. But something happened in the third century that hindered and blocked the flow of God's power. From that time until today, in the twenty-first century, we haven't seen that same demonstration of the true power of Pentecost with signs, wonders, and miracles being manifested.

God never intended for the power and anointing of the Holy Spirit which was released at Pentecost to diminish. He never intended for His miracle-working power or the gifts of the Spirit to cease to function within the Church. He intends for there to be a continual flow of His UNLIMITED, IMMEASURABLE POWER within His people today. **And most of all, God never intended Pentecost to be a one-time experience!!!**

God raised up the Church for a divine purpose. He raised up the Jews and manifested His supernatural power in their lives through signs, wonders, and miracles as a witness to show the world that Jehovah is the great I AM. He raised up the Church and placed His supernatural, miracle-working power within it as a witness to the world that Jesus is Who He claims to be, the Son of the Living God!

One of the major reasons why the Church today no longer has the full manifestation of power as it did during the first two centuries is because through the centuries, man has placed limitations upon God and the working of the Spirit.

Man has confined the **unlimited, immeasurable, POWER of GOD** within a structure based upon his natural, limited understanding, man-made traditions, and ideologies. God never intended to place any limitations upon His power and its manifestations within the Church. He also has not planned to put any limitations upon the release of His power through you!

Jesus said it is the *same* Spirit, not one that looks like the same Spirit, but actually *is* the same Spirit that raised Jesus from the dead.

> *But if the Spirit of him that raised up Jesus from the dead dwell in you, he that raised up Christ from the dead shall also quicken your mortal bodies by his Spirit that dwelleth in you.*
>
> Romans 8:11

God has destined you to be a man or woman of power and authority through Whom He manifests His supernatural power by healing the sick, casting out devils, raising the dead, and fulfilling His will in this end-time hour!

> *And suddenly there came a sound from heaven as of a rushing mighty wind, and it filled all the house where they were sitting. And there appeared unto them cloven tongues like as of fire, and it sat upon each of them. And they were all filled with the Holy Ghost, and began to speak with other tongues, as the Spirit gave them utterance.*
>
> Acts 2:2-4

The power came not in the beginning, when Jesus breathed on them and commanded them to receive it—but it came AFTER they had been seasoned and taught by the Lord Himself—after they had made the long journey from Passover to Pentecost. Remember, the disciples were not ready for the power when they had been in Jerusalem before and immediately after the crucifixion of Jesus.

Sitting in the Upper Room together in unity, praying, and waiting as the Lord had commanded them, they received the Holy

Spirit Whom Jesus had earlier commanded them to receive. And, as they did, the power was overwhelming. **This same power is available today for the life of any believer who is willing to step out in faith into this incredible promise.**

I must tell you, from the bottom of my heart, that we the Church have talked more about blessing ... we have emphasized more about tongues ... than we have about the **Person** of the Holy Spirit. I'm not against blessing. There are always awesome, incredible manifestations in service after service. But there's more. **God wants to take us past the point of blessing and into an experience of power!**

Our emphasis must be upon the Holy Spirit. The Holy Spirit is a **Person**! Our emphasis must not be on the gifts, the manifestations, or the outward expressions. When we emphasize outward manifestations instead of the precious Person of the Holy Spirit, we find there is an incredible, awesome lack. We've never gone past the point of blessing because we have overemphasized tongues and not the experience of power. At the point of blessing, people laugh in the Spirit, roll on the floor, and run the aisles. But, then they go home without power.

I hope you can come with me now deep in the Spirit. There is a reason why we do not have a true Pentecostal demonstration of power. One reason is because there is a lack of unity in the Church. The Word says, ... *they were all with one accord in one place* (Acts 2:1).

We are not talking about a denomination. Pentecost is not a denomination. We are not talking about the Assemblies of God, the Foursquare Church, the Church of God, Catholics, Greek Orthodox, or Charismatic independent churches. We are

talking about an experience. The power and manifestation is a result of a true encounter with the Holy Spirit. You are going to receive power, not because it's going to stand out there on a limb all by itself, **but because you have experienced the Person of the Holy Spirit.**

During the Charismatic renewal, something hit all denominations ... Baptists and Methodists ... Presbyterians and Roman Catholics. People were speaking in other tongues. A cry went up all over the world saying, "These people have received the Baptism of the Holy Spirit!"

An UNLIMITED POWER came upon the Church after this Pentecost experience. This power was the catalyst which produced signs and wonders among the unbelievers. It wasn't for the believers, it was for them who didn't believe.

Through healings, demons being cast out, and blind eyes being opened, an explosive manifestation of this power was displayed for the entire world to see Jesus—yes—Jesus, who He really was.

This infilling of power gave the Early Church a divine capability to produce the proof of the Resurrection of Jesus Christ, the Son of the living God. That same, exact Spirit that raised Jesus from the grave was the secret ingredient the allowed this Church to spread the Gospel!

Through this outpouring of the Holy Spirit and power, God raised up a NEW BREED of people ... a people walking in the POWER and AUTHORITY of Almighty God TO FULFILL HIS WILL upon the earth.

The 120 emerged from the Upper Room transformed from fearful, unbelieving, cowering, wavering disciples who had hidden behind closed doors, to fearless men and women who boldly declared the Gospel of Jesus Christ, with signs following.

No longer were they full of doubt, confused, or fearful. They had an experience of power ... they possessed a divine capability to do the same work Jesus had done. They knew this was their task. They began to boldly declare the Gospel in a demonstration of power.

I wonder where did the task of the Early Church change?

When Peter saw the lame man lying at the gate of the temple, he did not hesitate or waver. Hesitation is sin! He knew he had received the *dunamis* miracle-working power of God. He did not second guess what he should do. He spoke with power and authority, and commanding the man to rise in the Name of Jesus. He said,

> *... Silver and gold have I none; but such as I have give I thee: In the name of Jesus Christ of Nazareth rise up and walk.*

Acts 3:6

These were not the words of a man operating in his own strength, but these are the words of a Spirit-filled disciple operating in the power and authority of the Holy Spirit living within him. Peter didn't just decide to pray for this lame man, nor did he approach the man in his own limited abilities. HE WAS DIRECTED BY THE HOLY SPIRIT, and spoke under the unction of the power and authority of the Holy Spirit.

As Peter spoke the Word and lifted the man to his feet, the miracle power of God was released, and IMMEDIATELY the man was healed. He began leaping and walking, and entered into the temple, praising God! **Action ALWAYS follows faith-filled words.** Seeing is believing!

The rulers, elders, and high priests laid hands on Peter and John, and put them in prison. The next day, they gathered together, and brought Peter and John before them and demanded to know, ... *By what power, or by what name, have ye done this?* (Acts 4:7).

They knew it was not of Peter and John. Peter, full of the Holy Ghost, answered saying:

Be it known unto you all, and to all the people of Israel, that by the name of Jesus Christ of Nazareth, whom ye crucified, whom God raised from the dead, even by him doth this man stand here before you whole.

Acts 4:10

Not only did Peter preach that Jesus had been resurrected and that He was the only way by which man could be saved, but Peter produced the proof ... visible evidence ... that Jesus had been resurrected by speaking the word of healing in Jesus' Name. Peter focused his message upon the truth of Jesus' resurrection from the dead.

He told them, "We are witnesses!" In essence, Peter said, "We are witnesses of His resurrection. We produce EVIDENCE! Here it is ... this man standing before you in evidence. He was healed through faith in Jesus' Name!"

The Pharisees and high priests saw the man who had been lame from his mother's womb ... forty years ... made 100 percent whole. They could not deny that a great miracle had been manifested, but they refused to believe in Jesus, because they were still bound by the old ... the old formalism and old traditions of their religious dogma. They couldn't even recognize that God had done a mighty work in their midst. They were not ready to accept the new wine of the Holy Spirit God had poured out.

When Peter and John were commanded not to speak in the Name of Jesus, they didn't shrink from the conflict. They laid hold of the power of God within them. They looked the high priests and elders squarely in the face and said,

> ... *Whether it be right in the sight of God to hearken unto you more than unto God, judge ye. For we cannot but speak the things which we have seen and heard.*

> Acts 4:19-20

The fire of Pentecost was burning in them! The UNLIMITED POWER OF GOD was working within them, and this move of God could not be quenched!

Are you ready for God to ignite this Holy Ghost fire in your life? I believe that everything is going to change for you. This is your time to step into divine destiny! There is nothing as greater than to experience the promises of God operating in your life!

CHAPTER THREE

A FRESH BAPTISM OF THE HOLY SPIRIT

Over the years, the Church has quenched the moving of the Holy Spirit. But, today is a new day for the Church! It is a new beginning for you! God is ready to do a NEW WORK within the Church.

The *old wineskin* of the Church structure, which has been hindering the flow and demonstration of the power of God, is going to give way to the NEW!

God is going to pour out a powerful manifestation of the Holy Spirit! This could be setting up the Church for another Pentecost experience! God has been working in our lives ... preparing a NEW BREED of people ... for this end-time hour. He has been preparing us to release a fresh anointing of the Holy Spirit that calls for radical changes in our lives, in our way of thinking, in our way of living, in our way of ministering, and in our fulfilling His purposes.

Are you ready to draw a line on your past, to let go of the traditions holding you back from experiencing the fullness of the power of God flowing in your life? You must be willing to get rid of EVERY LIMITATION you have placed upon yourself and upon the flow of the power of the Holy Spirit in your life.

The power God wants to pour into your life is MASSIVE, ACTIVE, and VERY POTENT. It will revolutionize your entire life and ministry.

Don't be like the Pharisees, who missed the new move of God. They refused to embrace the power Jesus offered, because they were too bound to the old wine. God wants to give you a NEW ANOINTING of His Spirit. You cannot live off of an old anointing. It may have been sufficient for yesterday's challenges, but it won't work for today.

God wants to set your life on fire with the true power of Pentecost that will enable you to demonstrate and manifest the resurrection power of Jesus Christ to the world! And most of all, God wants to satisfy the longing of your life for a deeper relationship with your Lord.

Get ready for changes to happen within you and within your ministry. Be pliable in the hands of God, and allow Him to do whatever is necessary ... to cut away the things holding you back ... to purge and cleanse you of anything that would block the flow of His power and anointing through you.

As God begins to pour out this fresh Baptism of the Holy Spirit into your life, you will begin to move into a NEW DIMENSION of His power and authority. This will be a NEW DAY for your life! The time has come for the Church to rise up in the power and authority of Almighty God to push back the forces of darkness in the nations of the world, and proclaim the Gospel as a mighty, end-time witness of His UNLIMITED POWER!

Start now! Set aside time to get alone with God. Shut out everything else and just wait in His holy Presence.

Yield yourself totally to the working of His Spirit in your life. Ask God to do a New WORK within you. Don't withhold anything from the Lord.

As God does this new work in His people today, He is calling for a new consecration, a new dedication, and a new commitment! Draw a line on your past. **Rise up to a new level of dedication of all that you are and all that you have. Give yourself wholly and 100 percent to Him.**

God is doing a NEW WORK ... He is raising up A NEW BREED of people who are operating in His unlimited power to fulfill His will. He is ready to do a brand new work in your life. He is ready to pour out the *dunamis* power of His Spirit into you. Believe the Word of the Lord to you, today. Accept it by faith, and expect it to be manifested in your life as you yield yourself to Him!

Behold, the former things are come to pass, and new things do I declare: before they spring forth I tell you of them.

Isaiah 42:9

Behold, I will do a new thing; now it shall spring forth; shall ye not know it? I will even make a way in the wilderness, and rivers in the desert.

Isaiah 43:19

Thou hast heard, see all this; and will not ye declare it? I have shewed thee new things from this time, even hidden things, and thou didst not know them.

Isaiah 48:6

Once you embrace and partake in this Baptism of the Holy Spirit, God intends for you to have unlimited access to HIS resources which will position you to live above every obstacle and circumstance. After God fulfills that deep longing within you for His Spirit, you will be empowered to come against any attack that Satan will bring against you.

It is the anointing of the Holy Spirit that will break the yoke of bondage upon you and your unsaved loved ones. You can try everything you know to do in your own strength, but it won't do any good. It will take the anointing. It is the power of the anointing of the Holy Spirit that will make you victorious in the day-to-day circumstances that you face.

And it shall come to pass in that day, that his burden shall be taken away from off thy shoulder, and his yoke from off thy neck, AND THE YOKE SHALL BE DESTROYED BECAUSE OF THE ANOINTING.

Isaiah 10:27, emphasis added

Beloved, if Jesus felt it was necessary to take time to prepare Himself by having an experience of being filled with, and controlled by, the Holy Spirit before going out to face the enemy, then dare we do anything less? If He felt it was necessary to shut Himself away with God and to fast and pray, then it's time for us to do the same!

If the disciples spent ten days in the Upper Room interceding, and praying, it unveils the importance of coming before our Lord quietly, waiting on His Presence. Turn in your Bible and ask yourself, is this book truly the Word of God? If it is, does it have absolute authority over your life?

But ye shall receive power, after that the Holy Ghost is come upon you: and ye shall be witnesses unto me both in Jerusalem, and in all Judaea, and in Samaria, and unto the uttermost part of the earth.

Acts 1:8

The 120 emerged from the Upper Room totally transformed by their encounter with the Holy Spirit that God had released upon them. **They possessed a divine capability to do the work that God had commissioned them to do.** However, they couldn't just rely solely on that one experience to work the works of God from then on out.

They had to continually rely on the Spirit to lead, guide, and direct them. The same applies for you today. You must continually tap into your power source. (For more detailed reading on this subject, please refer to the section *Jesus Fulfillment of Pentecost*, in the Bible Study on page 41.

Your ability to stand in the authority of the power of the Holy Spirit is directly related to you continuing to have spiritual experiences. You must go past the point of blessing and enter into God's unlimited power for His Church. There is more to Pentecost than just doctrine. **There is an experience of POWER!**

This power has to be experienced continually. You can memorize doctrine, but doctrine will not give you what it takes to face the negative circumstances of this life and rise above mediocrity.

If ye then be risen with Christ, seek those things which are above, where Christ sitteth on the right hand of God.

Colossians 3:1

As you begin to read the Word of God and walk in the Spirit, you will be putty in the hands of the Maker. You're like clay; He has to shape and mold you. There are things in your life that may be displeasing to God, but as you begin to lay them on the altar, and as those carnal things depart from your life, they're replaced by the manifestation of the Spirit. **The more you yield and dedicate, the more you will get.** There are many gifts of the Spirit.

Somewhere between your birth and maturity, you receive the gift of tongues, and you speak in tongues, and then God will begin to use you in the gift of healing, for example. Then, maybe He will start using you in the gift of giving messages in other tongues, interpreting those tongues, or prophesying. Now, all of that can happen and your life still not be filled. Remember this gift is for you to. *Draw nigh to God and he will draw nigh to you* ... (James 4:8).

Can a person be filled with the Spirit and not baptized? There's where people don't have the spiritual breakthrough and understanding. It's possible for a person to be filled with the Spirit, but not be baptized. You say, how do you know, Brother Cerullo?

When I take an empty glass and pour water in, it contains water but isn't yet filled. The same is true spiritually. Just because you have received the gift of the Holy Spirit, doesn't mean your life is filled to overflowing with God's Spirit. Your life, like this glass, may by filled but not yet baptized. But, when I submerge this glass of water in a pitcher full of water, you can see that this vessel is now baptized.

God wants to so possess your life that His power and tangible presence overflow from you everywhere you go. You know that a vessel is filled when it is fully submerged in God to the extent your life has the Spirit without measure. **You can't measure it!**

Your spiritual experience is limited to the degree of your grasp of God's purpose and plan for your life. Let that statement sink down deep into your spirit. Think about it. When you were first born again, you were a newborn baby, spiritually. You had a limited understanding of God's purpose for your life. More than likely, you didn't fully understand what had happened to you.

Then, as you began to read and study God's Word, His Spirit began to remove the veil of darkness and unfold His plan and purpose for your life. The Spirit began to teach and guide you into all truth. (See John 16:13.) It was not until you began to grasp and lay hold of those promises, by faith, that you were brought into an experience of possessing and enjoying those promises.

For example, when the Holy Spirit reveals to you that it is His will for you to be healed, you must first release your faith and act on that promise before you have the experience of being healed.

REMEMBER,
ALL TRUTH IS PARALLEL!

Since Jesus is the Baptizer, anyone desiring to walk in the fullness of His power must continually come to the Source of the life-giving stream. A powerful example of our need of an intimate connection in scripture states, *Jesus stood and cried, saying, If any man thirst ... let him come unto me, and drink* (John 7:37).

All truth is parallel. So often many saints come before me saying, "Brother Cerullo, I want an overflow!" But I'm here to tell you, that before you begin to overflow, you must first be filled. Again, this instance isn't talking about a feeling or a sensation, it's talking about a spiritual infilling of power that must happen over and over again.

God wants you to come into an experience where you have been baptized—totally immersed—in the Holy Spirit. He has planned for you to face the enemy in the fullness of the Holy Spirit, as Jesus did. He has planned that the same *dunamis* power of the Holy Spirit that was manifested in Jesus' life will be manifested in your life.

He has also planned that you will remain full to overflowing with the Spirit. (For more detailed reading on this subject, please refer to the *Empowered from on High* section in the The Feast of Pentecost Bible Study on page 41, for more detailed reading on this subject.)

You know that to walk in the fullness of the Holy Spirit:

1. You must die to self.

2. You must yield to the Holy Spirit.

3. You must walk in the full knowledge of God.

To remain full and have a continual flow of the Holy Spirit in your life, you must keep your connection to the Spirit and yield yourself continually. Paul learned this great spiritual truth. He said, ... *I die daily* (I Corinthians 15:31).

People wondered if John the Baptist was the Christ, the promised Messiah. When they would come to him, asking if this was true, he would say: ... *I indeed baptize you with water; but one mightier than I cometh, the latchet of whose shoes I am not worthy to unloose: he shall baptize you with the Holy Ghost and with fire:* (Luke 3:16).

You must make it a priority to be immeasurably connected to the Baptizer! Your spiritual life depends on it!

CHAPTER FOUR

SIGNS AND WONDERS WILL FOLLOW

GOD NEVER INTENDED TO PLACE ANY LIMITATIONS UPON HIS POWER WITHIN THE CHURCH.

Over 2,000 years ago, Jesus' Church was birthed under the anointing of unlimited capability and unlimited power. However, something seemed to have happened during the second and third century. The Church lost that special ingredient which had allowed them to operate in this unlimited power.

Every time you lose the anointing and the free flow of the Holy Spirit, miracles and supernatural manifestation will cease. Yet, the Lord is heavily impressing upon my Spirit that there is coming a revival of true Pentecostal power. The same power that the Early Church had is going to be quickened to us once again.

Just as God did for the 120 in the Upper Room, you will no longer have doubt, be confused, or operate in fear. With this new manifestation of power, you will boldly declare the Gospel in a demonstration of power.

God's Word spoken with authority, invested in the promises of God will bring about the manifestation of God's spoken and written Word. This unlimited power will come upon you when you are truly baptized in the Holy Spirit. Are you ready for this power? I'm talking about coming into an experience of unlimited power that will totally change this world we live in.

The whole structure of the Church is going to change! And, you are going to see God use people ... everywhere ... in every way ... on the street corners, on your jobs, on the street where you live, and in your apartment building. With this Pentecostal experience comes power, and with this power comes relationship. And, with this relationship there will be no earthly force that can stop the work of the Lord from overtaking this generation.

Over the years, we have seen glimpses of revival, little shafts of light where a preacher is used to quicken a congregation full of believers. God is going to use His Church, not just a person. He's going to use the whole Church!

As a prophet of God, I prophesy to you that this is just the tip of the iceberg of what the Church will experience once they embrace the TRUE baptism in Holy Spirit! It will produce an immeasurable, unlimited result! **THIS will be the proof that we are the fulfillment of God's promise of Pentecost! Glory to GOD!**

How did the Early Church give witness? By the signs and wonders which were manifested through the power of the Holy Spirit flowing through them.

And by the hands of the apostles were many signs and wonders wrought among the people ...

Acts 5:12

God bore witness to them and the Gospel by the manifestation of His power.

God also bearing them witness, both with signs and wonders, and with divers miracles, and gifts of the Holy Ghost, according to his own will.

Hebrews 2:4

The true power of Pentecost was the power to proclaim the Gospel in a demonstration of power. As the disciples and believers exercised the power of the Holy Spirit to heal the sick, cast out devils, and raise the dead, they were giving **witness** to the resurrection of Jesus Christ ... providing undeniable proof that Jesus is Who He claims to be, the Son of the Living God!

The word *witness* is translated from the Greek word *Martus*. So many witnesses laid down their lives for their testimony about Jesus that the word *Martyr* gradually became understood as *one who bears witness by his death.* It was adopted into the English language as martyr. The word *witness* means *to give or to furnish evidence, one who demonstrates, substantiates, or verifies his testimony with an exhibition of evidence.*

The apostles and believers in the Early Church were witnesses, not simply by the words they spoke, but by the EVIDENCE they demonstrated through the signs and wonders, the lame walking, blind eyes being opened, demons cast out, and the dead raised, in the Name of Jesus.

35

They not only preached the Gospel, but they also DEMONSTRATED it! Paul said, ... *my speech and my preaching was not with enticing words of man's wisdom,* **but in demonstration of the Spirit and of power:** (I Corinthians 2:4, emphasis added).

Through the power of the Holy Spirit flowing through the Early Church the following things happened:

- **Signs and wonders were manifested!** *And fear came upon every soul: and many wonders and signs were done by the apostles* (Acts 2:43).

- **Multitudes were added to the Church!** *... believers were the more added to the Lord, multitudes both of men and women.* (Acts 5:14).

- **The sick were healed and devils were cast out!** *... they brought forth the sick into the streets, and laid them on beds and couches, that at the least the shadow of Peter passing by might overshadow some of them. There came also a multitude out of the cities round about unto Jerusalem, bringing sick folks, and them which were vexed with unclean spirits: and they were healed every one* (Acts 5:15-16).

As a result of the power of the Holy Spirit that was manifested in the Early Church, the Church spread out from Jerusalem, and in less than 35 years, capturing the very capital of the world, Rome itself!

In just 200 years, the Early Church, through the power and authority of the Holy Spirit working through the believers, was able to evangelize the entire known world with the Gospel. It was able to accomplish more in 200 years than the Church has accomplished in 2,000 years, including all of our modern technology!

The one thing that distinguishes the Church today from the Early Church is that the Early Church experienced a full demonstration and manifestation of the power of the Holy Spirit flowing through it, and today we don't!

> THE EARLY CHURCH TURNED
> THE WORLD UPSIDE DOWN, BECAUSE THEY
> HAD THE IMMEASURABLE, UNLIMITED
> POWER OF ALMIGHTY GOD
> FLOWING THROUGH THEM.

On the day of Pentecost, when the Holy Spirit came to dwell within them, they were changed! It was more than a celebration … more than just speaking in unknown tongues … more than an emotional experience. They did not have any preconceived ideas concerning what would happen, or how God would manifest His power in their lives.

God's Church will operate supernaturally. There is nothing about our Christian life that is natural. The miracle of creation was not natural. The death, burial, and resurrection, of Jesus Christ is not natural, the infilling of the Holy Spirit is not natural. Therefore, we cannot expect to see supernatural results when we attempt to operate under our strength.

God is ready to do a new work within the Church. This is not a time for the Church of Jesus Christ to relax, be at ease, slow down, or rest. Just as a runner receives a second wind, giving him a strong burst of energy to win the race, God is breathing a new, fresh wind of His Spirit upon the Church. This will cause us to surge forward in a greater demonstration of the power of God than we have ever experienced.

The world is going to know without a doubt that there is a miracle-working God, that there is power, healing, and cleansing in the Name of Jesus!

There is a tangible demonstration of power that the world will see once we reposition ourselves to embrace this revelation concerning the baptism of the Holy Spirit. Just as John prophesied in the Word of God that there was One coming Who was mightier than He—whose shoes He was unworthy to walk in. **HE would baptize them with the Holy Ghost and with fire!**

What will you do with the Baptism of the Holy Spirit? Just speak in tongues? Jump and shout? Get goose bumps? No! Ye shall receive POWER! The entire experience of Pentecost is about POWER! When the Church of today experiences this baptism, the world will witness the omnipotent, unlimited power of the Holy Spirit.

As we sit on the brink of the greatest demonstration of the power of God that this world has seen, my prayer is that this Baptism of the Holy Spirit would totally engulf your entire being!

A Special Word From MORRIS CERULLO

Partner, I have been in a special time of prayer interceding for God to release the power of Pentecost into your life like fresh fire! I don't want this season to pass by without you experiencing a tremendous outpouring of God's Spirit in your life.

God wants you to come before His Presence—His altar of Pentecost. Whatever hindrances, obstacles, and preconceived notions you've had of God, I want you to lay them on this altar! Allow His presence to remove fear and doubt from your mind.

The ingredient of God's unlimited POWER is what has fueled my entire ministry for more than six decades.

I couldn't have gone into the terrorist trenches of the world to declare the Gospel in my own strength and ability. I couldn't have visited every habitable continent in this world to lay hands on witchdoctors, warlocks, and Buddhists.

But through the Baptism of the Holy Spirit, God has empowered me to fulfill the very call He placed on my life in 1962, when He commissioned me saying, "Son, build Me an army!"

The death and resurrection of Jesus Christ had to take place before the Church could be formed. And, that same parallel truth applies today. There are things we must die to before we can step out in faith and receive the Baptism of the Holy Spirit.

Faith is fact, but faith is also an act! This Pentecost season, I dare you to step into your season of POWER—not just to feel good or go through a quickening of the Spirit. I dare you to ABIDE in this power, so you can work the works of God, producing the proof to this dying generation that Jesus is Who He says He is, to the glory of the Father!

Jesus' promise to you, today, is that ... *ye shall receive power* ... (Acts 1:8). Now that you have received this revelation into your spirit, it is now time for you to step into this experience of Holy Ghost power with me.

Your life, your family, your ministry, and this world will never be the same again!

Pray with me:

Dear Lord, the revelation of Your death and powerful resurrection is alive in my heart like never before! I pray, today, that You would baptize me afresh with your Holy Spirit. Let me move beyond just the shallow place of blessing, alone. Cause me to enter into a deeper relationship with You—to experience your POWER!

Today, I consecrate myself to Your will and Your ways. Let the FIRE of Pentecost burn mightily in my heart! Make me a witness for You. Release in me every gift of the Holy Spirit that You have destined to equip me with in order to reach this world for Jesus Christ!

Thank you, Lord! I now receive Your baptism. This is my appointed time to step in to a true experience of the POWER OF PENTECOST, in Jesus' Name!

Morris

MORRIS CERULLO BIBLE STUDY
THE FEAST OF PENTECOST

The Feast of Pentecost has been fulfilled!

- In the Feast of Passover, we see the death of Jesus.

- In the Feast of First Fruits, we see the resurrection of Jesus.

- In the Feast of Pentecost, we see the outpouring of the Holy Spirit, the New Covenant that we entered into with God, and the birth of a holy nation, the Church of the Living God!

When the day of Pentecost was fully come, Jesus fulfilled the Feast of Pentecost by sending the Holy Spirit to give birth to and empower His Church. At the divinely appointed time, God, sent the mighty outpouring of His Spirit.

ISRAEL'S CELEBRATION OF PENTECOST

The Feast of Pentecost (also called *the Feast of Weeks*, or, Shavuot) was one of seven feasts that God directed Israel to observe. Every year, every male, no matter where they lived, was required by law to travel to Jerusalem to attend three major feasts—Passover (which included the Feast of Unleavened Bread), Pentecost, and the Feast of Tabernacles. (See Deuteronomy 16:16.)

The Feast of Pentecost commemorated the giving of the Law and the covenant that God entered into with Israel on Mount Sinai. This signified the birth of the holy nation of Israel. It was **exactly fifty days** after God delivered them out of Egyptian bondage that He met with Moses on Mount Sinai.

On that day, the people heard the trumpet of God sound, summoning them together. He came down to meet with them and manifested His power and glory in fire and smoke on top of the mountain. They heard His voice and received the Law.

Fifty days from the day that the first fruits offering was waved before the Lord, the children of Israel celebrated the Feast of Pentecost. During this feast, before they harvested their grain crops, they dedicated the crops to God by waving two loaves of bread before the Lord and making offerings. (See Leviticus 23:15-18.) The two loaves of bread were the first fruits unto the Lord of their grain harvest.

The two loaves are a type of God's people. They are gathered by the Holy Spirit and presented to the Lord. On the Day of Pentecost, more than a thousand years after God met with the children of Israel on Mount Sinai, the Feast of Pentecost was fulfilled. God sent forth the Holy Spirit, and the Church was born.

JESUS' FULFILLMENT OF PENTECOST

The death and resurrection of Jesus had to be accomplished before the Church could be formed. After His resurrection, Jesus appeared and showed Himself through many infallible proofs. For forty days, He met with His disciples and gave them final instructions concerning the Kingdom of God before He ascended to heaven.

On the tenth day after that—**fifty days** after Jesus had risen from the dead, when the Day of Pentecost was fully come—120 disciples were assembled together. It was a divine appointment. God was to come down and meet with them.

Devout Jews (from all parts of Israel and the Mediterranean world) traveled to Jerusalem to attend these feasts. According to well-known Jewish historian Josephus, there were as many as 3 million Jews gathered in Jerusalem during the outpouring of the Holy Spirit on Pentecost.

As the crowds celebrated the Feast of Pentecost through the observance of the outward forms and rituals prescribed by the Law, in another part of the city, shut away in the Upper Room, 120 disciples experienced the **FULFILLMENT** of Pentecost. **The fire of God came down, and the Holy Spirit descended upon them in POWER!**

EMPOWERED FROM ON HIGH

The disciples received Jesus' promise and acted upon it. The doors were shut. The air was charged with a sense of expectancy. They had assembled together with one accord. They were waiting, believing, and expecting.

On that day, there was a **RELEASE** of God's supernatural POWER in their lives that enabled them to reach the world with the Gospel in just two hundred years. They were transformed from being fearful, unbelieving disciples into bold, fearless people of God who preached the Word in a demonstration of power.

The power of the Holy Spirit flowed through them to heal the sick, cast out devils, open blind eyes, and raise the dead! The

Church became a mighty moving force, a power that could not be shaken or defeated!

The Feast of Pentecost has been fulfilled! We no longer celebrate it through outward observances, of form, or rituals, but through lives that are fully yielded to God and empowered by the Holy Spirit. God wants to release His power within your life to enable you to do the same mighty works that Jesus did—and even greater works than these!

We celebrate the Feast of Pentecost today by proclaiming the Gospel in the same demonstration of power that the disciples and the Early Church manifested! God wants you to heal the sick, cast out devils, and raise the dead! Knowing that the power of the Holy Spirit is working within you, you are more than able to stand against **all** of the works of the enemy! **As Jesus had all power and authority over the devil, so do you, through the Holy Spirit!**

As God releases His power through you, and you move forward to penetrate the enemy's strongholds in your city and nation, there will be **NO POWER, NO EVIL FORCE, NO PRINCIPALITY,** and **NO WORK OF THE ENEMY** that will be able to defeat you!

If the enemy is attacking your finances, you do not have to be defeated! When you continue to walk in obedience to God and give, according to His will, you will be able to take authority over the power of the enemy. In the Name of Jesus, command the spirit of poverty over your life to be broken! Stand against the work of the enemy that tries to bind your finances. **Release your faith! Believe that God will release you from every financial bondage!**

God wants you, in this end-time hour, to live every day of your life in the power and anointing of the Holy Spirit. Walk in total victory over all of the power of the enemy. Ask God to release a fresh anointing of His Spirit upon you. Walk in God's power, and fulfill His will!

MY FAITH-PROMISE DECLARATION

Beloved, declare this out loud with me:

> *The Early Church was born in a demonstration of power! Jesus intends for me, as part of the Body of Christ, to have a supernatural experience with Him that causes me to walk in the same manifested demonstration of power as the Early Church. Signs and wonders will follow me as I yield to His Spirit and walk in the power of His Word.*

Dr. Morris Cerullo
A Man of Vision

Dr. Morris Cerullo is respected and revered by millions around the world. He has sacrificially dedicated his life to helping hurting people and to taking the good news of salvation to the nations. As a worldwide evangelist and a father of the faith to many of today's renowned spiritual leaders, his life has been an inspiration to many.

Affectionately known as 'Papa', Morris is also a prophetic voice who has personally trained more than 3 million Christian leaders, otherwise known as Nationals, around the world to reach their own countries for Jesus Christ.

In 1962, Morris Cerullo received divine instructions from God: "Son, build Me an army." God revealed to him that the spiritual key to building His army would be to train lay people— doctors, lawyers, ditch diggers, plumbers, farmers, ranchers, carpenters, housewives, sailors, factory workers, household servants—everyone is a potential minister.

This God-given vision of reaching multiplied millions for the Gospel is now being fulfilled through the building of a worldwide, state-of-the-art, training center. The Morris Cerullo Legacy International Center will offer ministerial training for ordination, individual course training, as well as Bible prophecy and Hebrew studies.

Morris Cerullo's passion has further blossomed into the launch of a revolutionary, seven-year campaign: the **20/20 Vision**. With the goal of reaching **20 million souls** and training **20 million Nationals** by the year **2020**, the purpose of the **20/20 Vision** is to reach the entire world with the Gospel through the training and equipping of these Nationals.

Dr. Cerullo is a prolific author of more than 200 classic Christian books, and unique study Bibles. He has also produced an abundance of training materials on DVD.

Learn more about Morris Cerullo and the **20/20 Vision** at our Web site, **www.mcwe.com.**

United States
P. O. Box 85277 • San Diego, CA 92186
(858) 277-2200

United Kingdom
P. O. Box 277 • Hemel Hempstead, Herts HP2 7DH
(01442) 232-432

Canada
P. O. Box 3600 • Concord, Ontario, L4K 1B6
(905) 669-1788
Web site: www.mcwe.ca

 www.facebook.com/officialmorriscerullo

 twitter.com/morris_cerullo

 www.youtube.com/DrMorrisCerullo

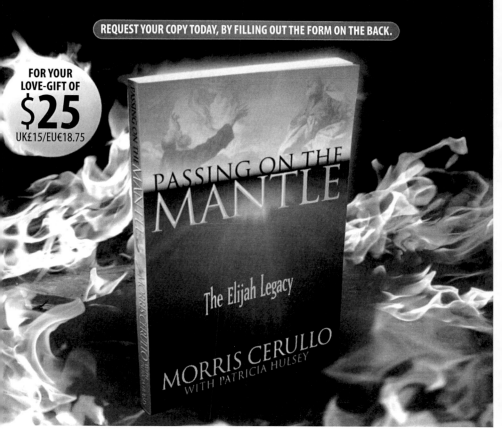

ORDER FORM

❑ **Yes, Brother Cerullo!** I am ready to receive the mantle of anointing and work the works of God! Please send me _____ copies of *Passing on the Mantle* (B410). I've enclosed **$25 (UK£15/EU€18.75)** for each copy.

Total enclosed: $/£/€ _____.

❑ **Please pray for the following needs in my life to be met:**

_____

_____

_____

_____

_____

_____

_____

_____

_____

❑ MR. & MRS.　　❑ MR.　　❑ MRS.　　❑ MS.　　❑ MISS

NAME | | | | | | | | | | | | | | | | | | | | | | | |

ADDRESS | | | | | | | | | | | | | | | | | | | | | |

CITY | | | | | | | | | | | | | | | STATE OR PROVINCE | | | | | | | |

ZIP/POSTAL CODE | | | | | | | COUNTRY | | | | | | | |

❑ Cell ❑ Home
TELEPHONE | | | | - | | | - | | | | E-MAIL | | | | | | | |
AREA CODE

IF USING A CREDIT CARD, BE SURE TO SIGN YOUR NAME AND INCLUDE EXPIRATION DATE.

I AM PAYING BY: | | | | | | | | | | | | | | | | | | | | | - | | |

CARD NUMBER　　　　　　　　　　　　　　　　EXPIRATION DATE

❑ MASTER CARD/ACCESS　❑ VISA　❑ AMERICAN EXPRESS　❑ DISCOVER　❑ MAESTRO　Security Code　❑ SWITCH　Switch Issue No.

NAME: _____

(Please print your name as it appears on your card)

SIGNATURE: _____

MORRIS CERULLO WORLD EVANGELISM · **Web site:** www.mcwe.com
U.S.: P.O. Box 85277, San Diego, CA 92186 · **Tel:** (858) 633-4885
U.K.: P.O. Box 277, Hemel Hempstead, Herts HP2 7DH · **Tel:** 44(0)1442-232432
CAN.: P.O. Box 3600, Concord, Ontario L4K 1B6 · **Tel:** (905) 669-1788
CAN. Web site: www.mcwe.ca

25077